Young Learner's

HOW TO DRAW

Step by Step

Young Learner Publications®
G-1A Rattan Jyoti, 18 Rajendra Place, New Delhi- 110 008 (INDIA)
Tel: 25750801, 25820556, 25755559 Fax: 91-11-25764396
Website: www.goodwillpublishinghouse.com
E-mail: gph.ylp@goodwillpublishinghouse.com
goodwillpub@gmail.com

Animal Figures

In this exercise, we will draw animals with the help of basic shapes. The first step is to observe the outer shape of the animal's body and then think which basic shape will fit best in which part of the body. An animal's body is drawn using several shapes as shown below in the camel drawing.

Carefully follow all the steps of drawing the camel. Draw using a lead pencil and colour with crayons in the boxes given below.

1	2	3

Carefully follow all the steps of drawing the dog and the cat. Draw using a lead pencil and colour with crayons in the boxes given below.

1	2	3

1	2	3

1	2	3

1	2	3

Carefully follow all the steps of drawing the rabbit and the cow. Draw using a lead pencil and colour with crayons in the boxes given below.

1	2	3

1	2	3

1	2	3

1	2	3

Carefully follow all the steps of drawing the giraffe. Draw using a lead pencil and colour with crayons in the boxes given alongside.

1	1
2	2
3	3

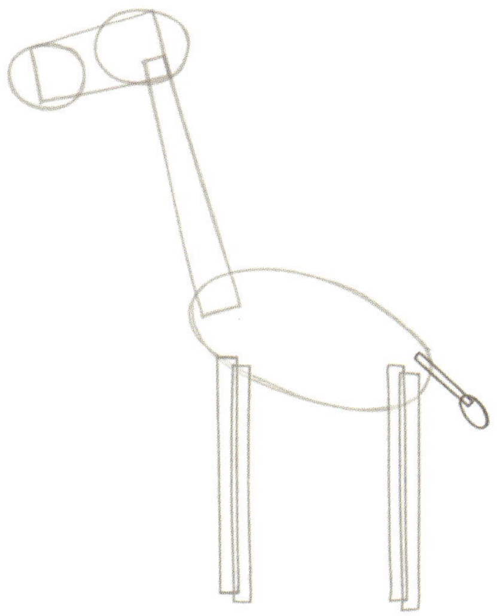

Carefully follow all the steps of drawing the elephant. Draw using a lead pencil and colour with crayons in the boxes given alongside.

1

1

2

2

3

3

Carefully follow all the steps of drawing the lion. Draw using a lead pencil and colour with crayons in the boxes given alongside.

1 	1
2 	2
3 	3

Carefully follow all the steps of drawing the horse. Draw using a lead pencil and colour with crayons in the boxes given alongside.

1

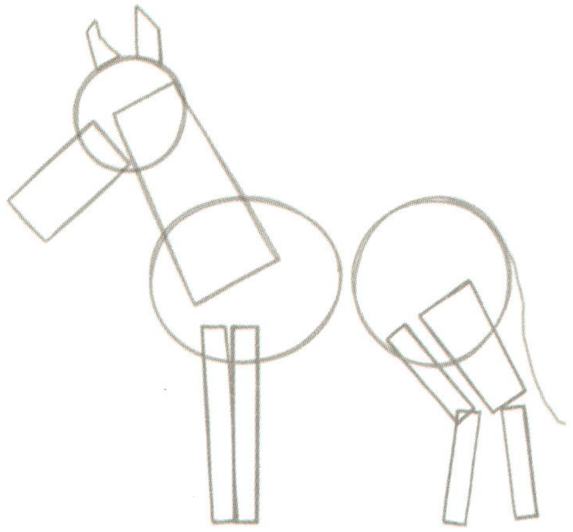

2

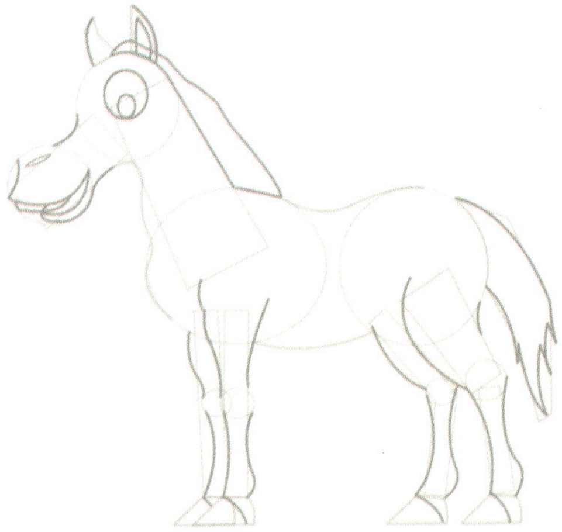

3

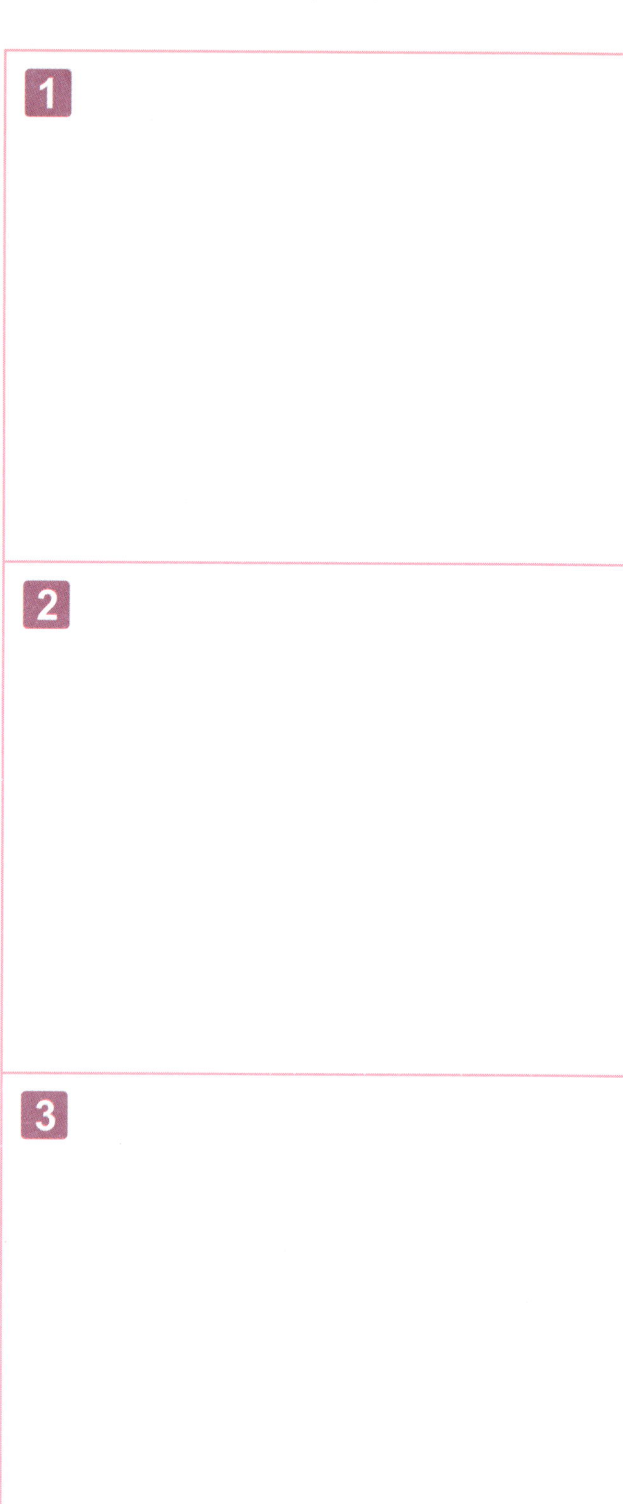

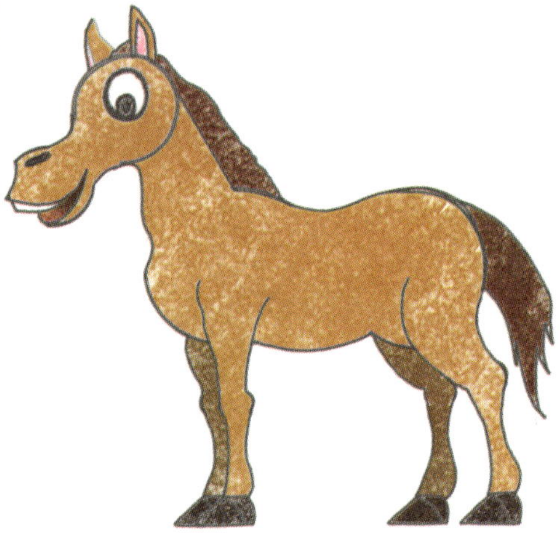

1

2

3

For teachers and parents: Besides this exercise, encourage the children to practise drawing other animals in their sketchbooks using this technique.

Simple Cartoon Figures

In this exercise we will practise drawing simple cartoon figures. We will use basic shapes for simplifying the form of the cartoon figures.

Follow each step of drawing the kid's face carefully. Draw using a lead pencil and colour with crayons in the boxes given below.

1	2	3

Follow each step of drawing the girl carefully. Draw using a lead pencil and colour with crayons in the boxes given below.

1	2	3	4

Follow each step of drawing the boy carefully. Draw using a lead pencil and colour with crayons in the boxes given below.

1	2	3

Follow each step of drawing the young man carefully. Draw using a lead pencil and colour with crayons in the boxes given below.

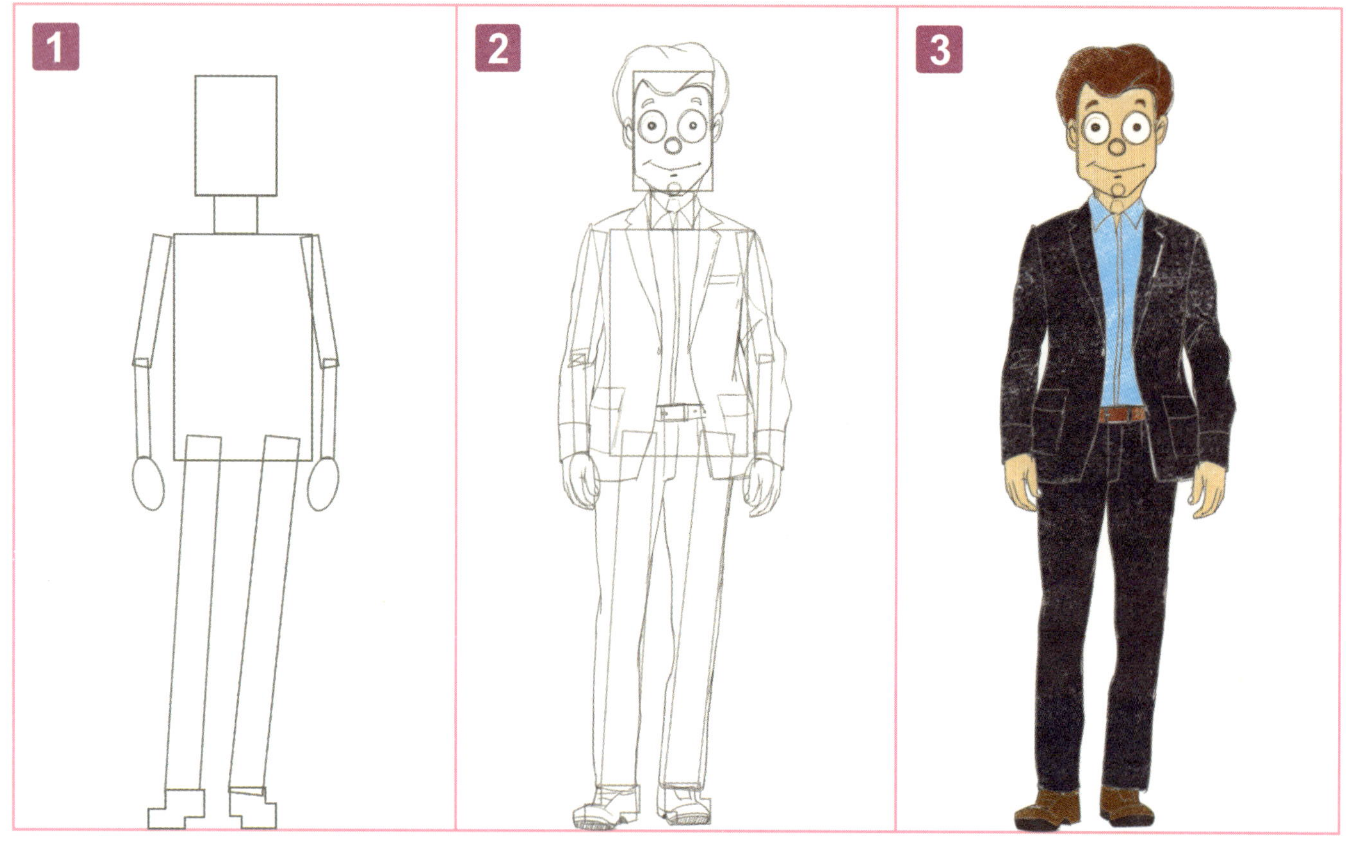

1

2

3

Follow each step of drawing the young woman carefully. Draw using a lead pencil and colour with crayons in the boxes given below.

1	2	3

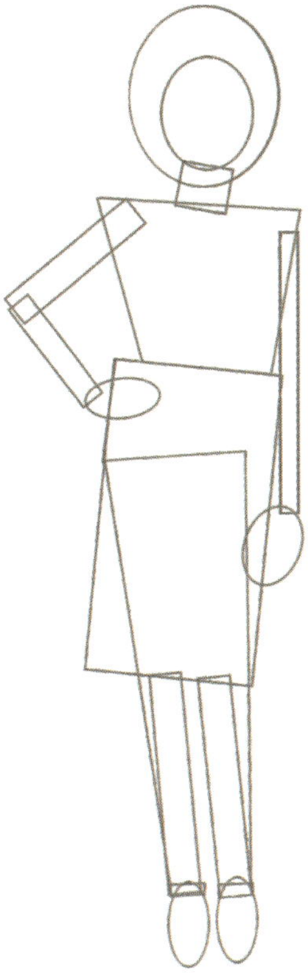

1	2	3

Follow each step of drawing the old man carefully. Draw using a lead pencil and colour with crayons in the boxes given below.

1	2	3

Follow each step of drawing the old woman carefully. Draw using a lead pencil and colour with crayons in the boxes given below.

1

2

3

1

2

3

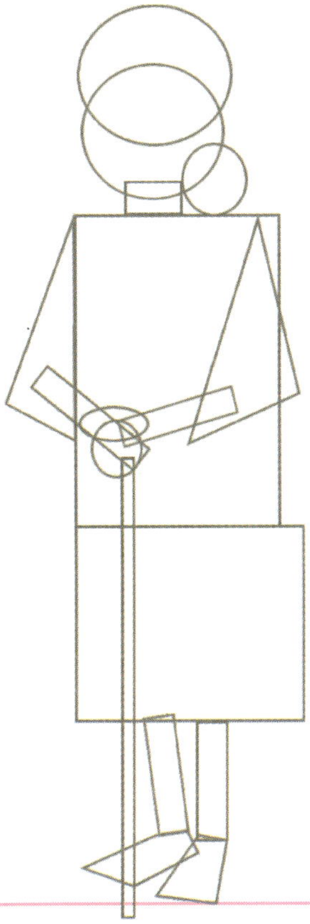

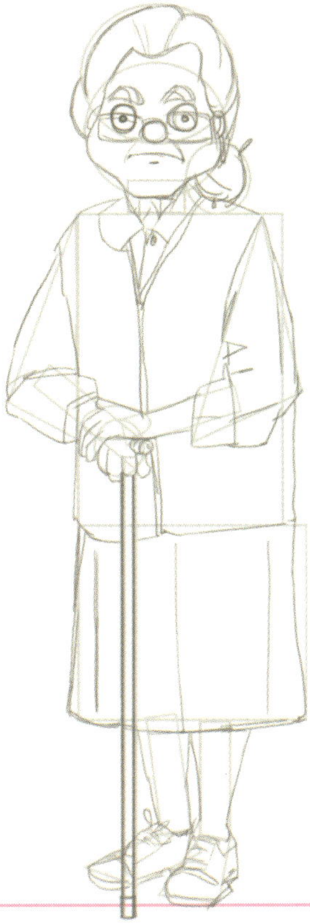

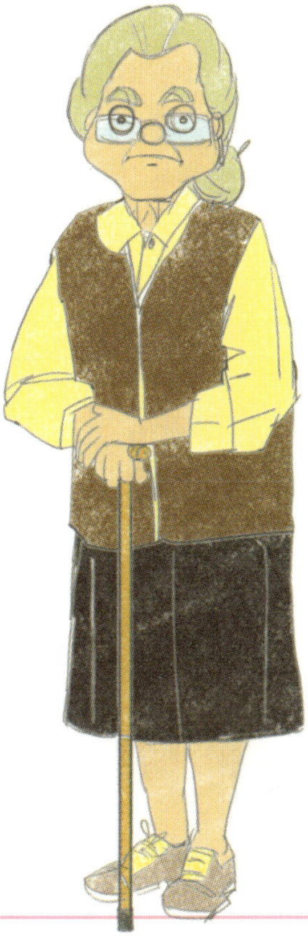

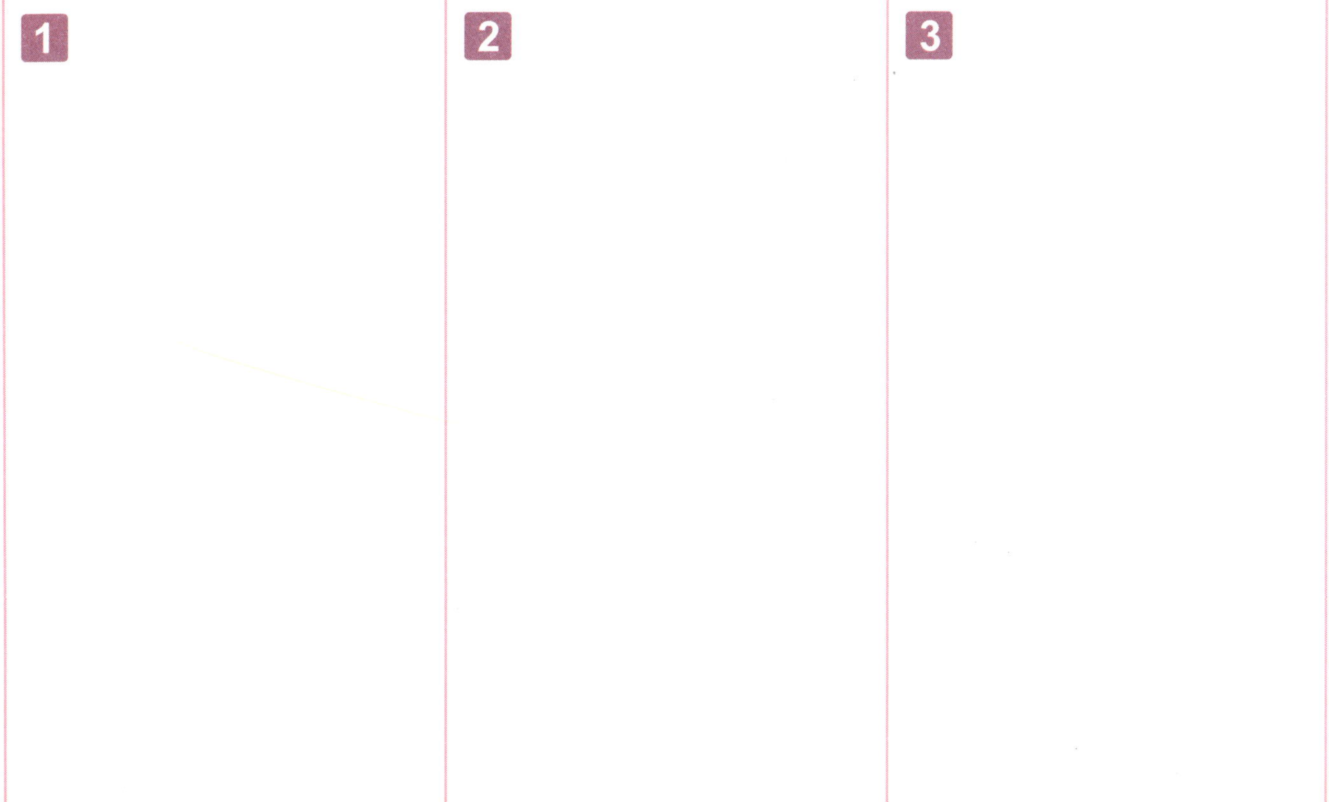

Complete the family composition using a lead pencil and colour with crayons in the box given below. The first step has been done for you.

For teachers and parents: Besides this exercise, encourage the children to practise drawing different postures of their family members in their sketchbooks by using the same technique.